MW00790678

Fences and Walls

Focus: Designing, Making and Appraising

PETER SLOAN &
SHERYL SLOAN

Fences and walls are made to keep people and animals in or out.

People have fences around their yards and swimming pools. The fences keep pets and children safe. The fences stop people and animals from getting in.

The tiger has its own
yard at the zoo.
Around the tiger's yard
is a high fence.
Around the fence there
is a deep moat.
Around the moat is a
fence to keep people out.

4

A walkway over a busy
highway has a steel
fence. Sometimes it is
covered with wire.
The fence stops people
from falling over the
side onto the highway.

Some factories have very high walls around their yards. The walls have big gates to let trucks in and out. The walls stop people from entering the factories.

6

People like to watch big
buildings being built.
The builders put up a
wall or fence to stop
the people getting in
the way. Sometimes they
put windows in the wall
so people can watch
safely.

Farmers put fences
around their fields.
The fences keep the
farm animals from
straying. They also keep
people and animals out
of fields planted with
crops.